What I Tell Myself

ABOUT TALENT

Written by Michael A. Brown • Illustrated by Lovyaa Garg

This book is dedicated to...

My children and all children who should explore the beauty of childhood and talent expression.

What I Tell Myself About Talent Copyright © 2020 by Michael A. Brown, MA. All rights reserved. Printed in the United States of America. No part of this book may be used or reproduced in any manner whatsoever without permission from the author. For information address the author at info@whatitellmyselffirst.com. Visit the official website at www.WhatITellMyselfFirst.com.

First Edition

Edited by Michele L. Mathews

Illustration by Lovyaa Garg

Design by Zoe Ranucci, www.GoodDharma.com

ISBN: 978-1-7352024-1-9

Library of Congress Control Number: 2020911640

About the Author

Born in Chicago, IL, Michael A. (Mike) Brown, MA is the author of a revolutionary social emotional children's book series, What I Tell Myself, beginning with What I Tell Myself FIRST: Children's Real-World Affirmations of Self-Esteem. Based on Maslow's Hierarchy of Needs, this book of real-world affirmations highlights the various abilities and attributes of the reader while exposing readers to realistic possibilities of rejection of difference in various forms thereby enabling readers to form mental frameworks to surmount those forms of rejection and achieve positive self-actualization. Mr. Brown continues the mission to heal and empower all with the What I Tell Myself series of books.

Also from Michael A. Brown

What I Tell Myself FIRST *is on a mission to heal kids and parents!* **Real-world affirmations WORK!** Like the AED is to a heart, this book instills the defibrillator of self-esteem. So powerful that it addresses bullying and outside attacks on the self by other people who need the very same help themselves. For when times are tough and your mind is under attack, reality-based daily affirmations are the "I wish I had this" of books.

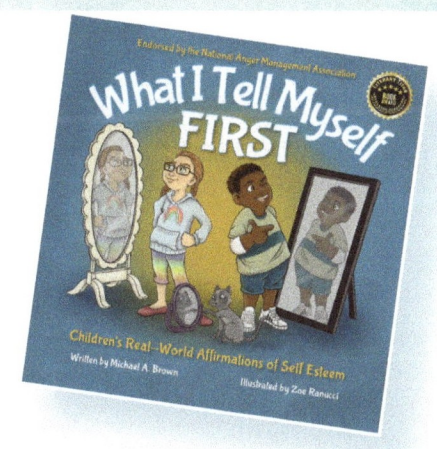

What I Tell Myself About Self–Protection *is continuing the mission to heal and empower adults, parents, grandparents, children, caretakers, crime victims, and others inspiring readers to take an active approach to self-protection against active threats and deadly threatening situations.* From declaring one's right to be free and grow to being situationally aware, this book guides readers to take strong decisive actions and empower their loved ones or those in their care to do the same. Whether there's danger head or imminently present, it is NO ONE's job to protect you. It is your job. Be. Know. Do. Survive.

www.WhatITellMyselfFirst.com

Talent is what some may say
I'll be good at this someday.

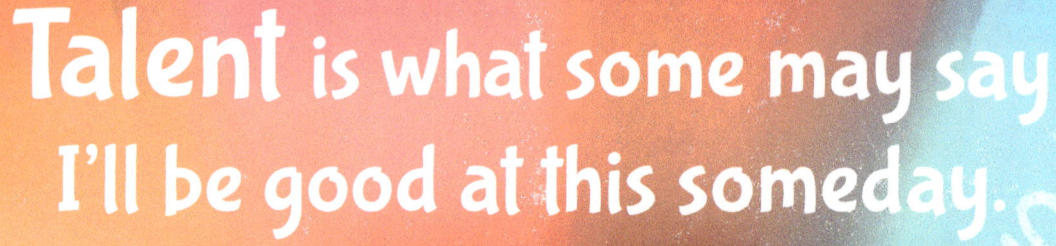

BRAVO!
SO GOOD!
AMAZING!
WOW!

But what is it I like to do?
Let's explore! Let's pursue!

I collect my teddy bears.
Check their hearts and give them care.

I sure hope they feel alright.
What can I be in this life?

Sing along, sing a song.
Sing with Maddy all day long.

♫ La–La–La ♫ Come sing with me!
What is my favorite song to sing?

Pots and pans. Taps and bangs.
Rat–ta–tat–tat–tat–ting

Fall in line. Keep the time.
What can I be in due time?

Find a corner. Grab a seat.
Kick up my HAPPY feet!

Pick it up. Give it a look!
What is my most FAVORITE book?

Love to write?
Love to draw?
Love to paint?

I'll try it ALL!

Rolling fast down the court.

Swimming swiftly in my lane.

Bouncing hard or swimming fast.
We play hard through the pain.

Yes! First place is the goal!
Can't make it 'til you try.

What we play, we really like!
Hmmmm.... What sports have I tried?

Stack 'em up.
Stack 'em high.

Build a tower
to the sky.

Builder Bobby, tried and true!
What can I build with his crew?

Candy bags.
Gummy chews.

What can I be to you?

I make you laugh with your friends.
I dance and sing. I wear your things.

And when you share, I get good views!
When I grow up, what will I choose?

All our life,
we've watched you.

When you march,
we march, too.

When you see us, you salute!

You wear green. Can I? Me, too?

Never know what I can do.

Until I try. Until I do.

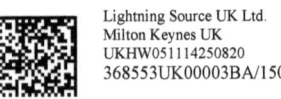

Lightning Source UK Ltd.
Milton Keynes UK
UKHW051114250820
368553UK00003BA/150